Ever Ancient, Ever New

Structures of Communion in the Church

ARCHBISHOP John R. Quinn

D0898279

Paulist Press
New York / Mahwah, NJ

Cover image copyright by nhtg/Shutterstock.com
Cover and book design by Lynn Else

Library of Congress Cataloging-in-Publication Data

Quinn, John R. (John Raphael), 1929–
    Ever ancient, ever new : structures of communion in the church / John R. Quinn.
    pages cm
    ISBN 978-0-8091-4826-4 (alk. paper) — ISBN 978-1-58768-235-3
1. Church. 2. Catholic Church—Doctrines. I. Title.
    BX1746.Q56 2013
    262'.02—dc23

                                                        2012042344

ISBN: 978-0-8091-4826-4 (paperback)
ISBN: 978-1-58768-235-3 (e-book)

Published by Paulist Press
997 Macarthur Boulevard
Mahwah, New Jersey 07430

www.paulistpress.com

Printed and bound in the
United States of America

CONTENTS

INTRODUCTION

Communion in the Church is not simply a feeling or an abstraction. It is a manifestation of the mystery of the Most Holy Trinity revealed in Christ Jesus our Lord and accomplished through the Spirit of the Father and the Son. Yet as an earthly and visible reality, communion requires a structure. In this book, I deal with the fact that the Church from its inception thought of itself as a communion and then expand upon the development of the great historic structures of communion: synods, patriarchates, and councils. My point is that these collegial structures of communion have opened a path today for the Latin Church to remedy what Joseph Ratzinger once called "extreme centralization."[1]

I have occasion to cite Ratzinger at various points in this book and use three different methods of reference. I refer to the earlier theologian-professor as Joseph Ratzinger. The Prefect of the Congregation for the Doctrine of the Faith I refer to as Cardinal Ratzinger. Any later reference, of course, will be to Pope Benedict XVI.

My deep-felt gratitude goes to Francis A. Sullivan, SJ, who so generously agreed to read the manuscript, made important and substantive comments, and bore patiently with my limitations. My great thanks go to Father Milton Walsh who did research for me and assisted me throughout the writing of this book. I also thank Archbishop Stefan Soroka of the Ukrainian Archeparchy of Philadelphia and Ronald G. Roberson, CSP,

Associate Director of the staff of the Bishops' Committee on Ecumenical and Interreligious Affairs of the USCCB, for their observations surrounding my chapters on the patriarchates. To Michael J. Buckley, SJ, I am grateful for the extremely helpful textual comments, and to my secretary, Linda Asti, I express my continuing appreciation.

CHAPTER 1

THE CHURCH:
A COMMUNION FROM THE BEGINNING

The Church, as we see it in the pages of the New Testament, had a clear consciousness that it was a communion. It was not a group of isolated, independent communities.[1] Nor has there been any evidence that the original communities were first independent groups, which later federated into a single Church.[2] Instead, specific bonds joined these multiple communities into one Church from the beginning. At the level of doctrine, for instance, there was the fundamental conviction that all the churches had to be faithful to the original witness and teaching of the apostles as indicated in Acts: "They devoted themselves to the apostles' teaching…" (2:42). This meant that they held fast to that teaching with persistent tenacity.[3] And because all the churches belonged to one Lord, embraced one faith, and were brought into being by one baptism, their members were brothers and sisters to one another. Consequently, at the level of service, they had some responsibility for one another. They expressed this by helping the poor in other churches and by offering hospitality to visitors and travelers from other churches. Paul, for instance, gives a lengthy exhortation to his Corinthian community regarding a collection for the poor in Jerusalem (2 Cor 9:1–15). Also, the Letter to the Hebrews urges believers, "Let mutual love continue. Do not neglect to show hospitality to strangers, for by doing that some have entertained angels without knowing it" (Heb 13:1–2). The many churches knew that they were one Church: "There is one body and one Spirit, just as you were called to the one hope that belongs to your calling, one Lord, one faith, one baptism, one God and Father of us all…" (Eph 4:4–6). To say this is to say that the original Christians had a sense of communion. There was more than mere friendship among people who knew each other. Communion linked people in Jerusalem and Corinth, in Galatia and Colossae, who did not have personal contact with one another. Communion meant that all these communities—scattered in various places and possessing diverse cultures—acknowledged the same Lord, Jesus Christ, celebrated the same Eucharist, held and handed on the same Word (they shared certain valued and precious realities). "This 'having the same things in common' forms a bond of unity among those who share them and is the foundation of the concept of *koinonia*, or 'communion.'"[4]

One New Testament instance that dramatically tested ecclesial communion but at the same time revealed its nature, is the blazing controversy over whether Gentile converts should be required to observe the Law of Moses, in particular, the dietary laws and the religious rite of circumcision. This controversy came to a head when some Jewish Christians visiting Paul's communities vigorously protested against his insistence that the obligation of circumcision and other ritual prescriptions of the Mosaic Law were not to be imposed on Gentile converts for the reason that salvation lay in Jesus Christ and in his saving Passion, Death, and Resurrection, not in the observance of the Mosaic Law.[5] These Jewish Christians forthrightly declared, "Unless you are circumcised according to the custom of Moses, you cannot be saved" (Acts 15:1).

And so we must ask these questions: How did the Church

resolve this problem? How did it preserve communion in the face of such serious differences? Looking into the New Testament, we see that there were three factors involved in settling the problem: pastoral experience, the appeal to Scripture, and the Jerusalem meeting of the leaders. No one of these three factors alone determined the solution; they were all interrelated.

The relationship between doctrine and pastoral experience was of crucial importance.[6] The solution to the controversy did not come simply from an abstract examination of doctrinal principles. It was through and in the pastoral experience of the exemplary Christian life of the Gentiles whom Paul baptized without the requirement of circumcision, and of the outpouring of the Spirit on Cornelius and his Gentile friends as soon as Peter had preached the Gospel to them (Acts 10),[7] that a singularly important doctrinal development took place in the Church. This doctrinal development occurred because the Church discerned between God working in the existential situation of the Church and her actual experience. Further, the searing controversy over the freedom of Gentile Christians from the Law powerfully dramatized that discernment is not easy. In this New Testament concern, the plan of God for the Church was discerned only after long, arduous search and controversy. The path was not self-evident.

This crisis of the primitive Church stands as a perpetual warning to the Church of every age that it cannot expect to find easy or quick solutions to its doctrinal and pastoral problems any more than the primitive Church did. Authentic discernment calls for evangelical patience, for openness to do the will of God, and for humble listening for the voice of God.

But the pastoral experience of Peter and Paul was not an independent factor. They were conscious of the normative character of the Scriptures. Consequently, it was the painstaking discernment of the pastoral experience in light of the Scriptures and discernment of the Scriptures in light of the pastoral experience, which led to clarity about the place of the Mosaic Law and the absolute centrality of Christ. This, in fact, is what James does in his speech at this assembly—he refers to the prophets and cites Amos as foretelling that the gentiles will come to be called God's people (Acts 15:13–21).[8]

The third element in resolving the problem is the actual meeting in Jerusalem, which showed that such serious questions of doctrine and practice were not to be settled by Scripture or pastoral practice taken separately. They were not to be settled by one apostle alone or by one independent church community. The questions were to be resolved in communion with the whole Church. And so, Paul went up to Jerusalem to see "the apostles and the elders" (Acts 15:2). He had the conviction that whatever he was doing and teaching ultimately had to be in harmony with the teaching and practice of the apostles at Jerusalem; his ministry and preaching had to be in communion. "Then I laid before them (though only…with the acknowledged leaders) the gospel that I proclaim among the Gentiles, in order to make sure that I was not running, or had not run, in vain" (Gal 2:2). Paul had the humility to admit that he could have "run in vain," and he knew that if the mother church in Jerusalem denied him communion, his breaking communion and going his own way would negate the very nature of the Church.[9] Paul is not narrowly or exclusively fixated on his practice of exempting gentile converts from the Jewish law. He also has the larger perspective about preserving unity and communion in the Church—an example not to be forgotten in the fervor of some modern controversies. Also, we should be aware that Paul does not seek definitive resolution of this grave problem from the Jerusalem community as such but from "the acknowledged leaders." Both Peter and Paul had the unshakable conviction that the crucified Lord had indeed risen from the dead and was continually present and working in the Church. And it became clear to them that the risen Lord was, in fact, working in gentile Christians who did not observe the Mosaic Law.

Joseph Fitzmeyer sees in the Jerusalem meeting a seminal form and structure, which later led to councils in the Church.[10] The decision of the apostles and leaders in Acts is also a strong witness that unity in faith is compatible with important differences in practice and shows that there is room for diversity, even on matters of major importance, within the framework of unity.

This consciousness of the essential need to preserve communion among the believers and the communities endured in the Church after the death of the apostles. St. Ignatius of Antioch, martyred around the year 110, speaks in his letters of the episcopal structure as widespread by that time. By the middle of the second century, Christian communities were commonly organized with a single bishop as leader. The instinct for unity and the consciousness of communion appeared not only in the episcopal structure adopted in the churches, but also in the way of choosing bishops in the Church. Bishops were chosen by their church communities, but there was also a wider participation of the Church, particularly the neighboring communities. The choice of a bishop was a matter of concern not only to one individual church but to the Church as a whole. The bishop was not simply the leader of a local community. He was a member of the Apostolic College: a bishop in communion with the other bishops because his church was in communion with the other churches. Still another indication of belonging to a communion in which all the churches were one Church, appeared in the requirement that bishops from the other churches should take part in the ordination of a bishop. Consequently, at the Council of Nicaea (AD 325), it was decreed that a bishop should be appointed by all the bishops of the province and if all were unable to participate in the actual ordination, at least three should perform the ceremony.[11] This prescription of Nicaea was not an innovation and did not begin at Nicaea. The Council of Nicaea simply confirmed and gave direction to a practice that already existed.[12]

Communion, as the requirements for ordination show, meant that there was a reciprocity and mutuality among the bishops and their churches. Important expressions of this were the letters of communion common among bishops and churches in antiquity.[13] Whenever a Christian traveled, he carried with him a letter from his own bishop stating that he was a member of that local church community. With such a letter, the traveler would then be welcomed to the Eucharist in the various church communities he might visit on his travels. In addition, the communities and the bishop would give the traveler hospitality during his stay. The bishops in this period also kept lists of all the churches in the world with which they were in communion and a letter of communion was only valid if it came from a bishop on that list. These lists, of course, had to be revised as bishops died or lapsed into heresy. Notices of death or censure were, thus, sent to all the bishops as well as notice of the election of a new bishop. The fact that Tertullian[14] makes reference to this practice indicates that it existed very early and is another intimation that the pre-Nicene Church had a clear sense that it was a communion of churches. The process of bishop selection and ordination, the resolution of problems concerning church practice and doctrine (as in the case of the Mosaic Law controversy), and the practice of keeping lists of all the bishops in the world and issuing letters of communion all showed a consciousness of the Church as one Church and a consciousness that all these churches were in communion. Very early, even before Nicaea, there is evidence of the existence of structures of communion, of communication and interdependence by which the Church was persevered in unity and in the apostolic heritage.[15]

One of the earliest structures of communion were synods.[16] These were meetings the bishops of a region held (beginning at least 150 years before the Council of Nicaea) to deliberate about common concerns and problems.[17] From the early synodal structure of the ancient Church, there came two other important structures of governance and communion: the metropolitan structure and the patriarchal structure. The next chapters will deal with the rise of synods in the Church as well as the development of the metropolitan and patriarchal structures in the Church.

CHAPTER 2

STRUCTURES OF COMMUNION: SYNODS

Communion, if it is not to remain an abstraction, has to have a concrete shape and structure. The Church is a visible and sacramental reality and therefore, "requires that collegial unity be expressed not only in events but in enduring, visible, locally rooted collegial structures and institutions."[1] One of the very earliest structures of communion were synods, meetings of the bishops of a region convened to deliberate about common concerns and problems (doctrinal, liturgical, and disciplinary).

Synods were already being held at least 150 years before the Council of Nicaea. The synods of antiquity show clear affinities with the Jerusalem Council of Acts 15. Like the Jerusalem meeting, in the synods, there is a problem to be solved: dissension within the community gives rise to an assembly of the leaders, discourses express differing views on the subject, a decision is expressed in a synodal decree, and community acceptance of the decision is reached.[2]

The first clearly attested synod was held in the year AD 175 to deal with the Montanist heresy.[3] This heresy, named after its leader, Montanus, may be described in simple terms as a combination of severity and exuberance. It was excessively rigorous in moral and ascetical matters, requiring married people to separate or to live in continence. On the other hand, its adherents indulged in demonstrative displays of alleged invasion by the Holy Spirit. Thus, there was widespread shock when the learned apologist of the Christian faith, Tertullian, embraced Montanism. Ronald Knox said, "It was as if Newman had joined the Salvation Army."[4]

In the same century, a growing problem was created by the existence of different traditions regarding the day for the celebration of Easter. The churches in the Roman Province of Asia celebrated it on the same day as the Jewish Passover, which was not always a Sunday; while most other churches, including Rome, celebrated it on Sunday. Around the year 150, there was a discussion between Pope Anicetus and Polycarp, the Bishop of Smyrna (a church of the Province of Asia). Polycarp's insistence on maintaining the custom of his province caused no break of communion between them. However, the problem became more acute when Christians who came from that province to Rome settled together and formed house-churches in which they maintained their own different custom regarding Easter, causing disunity in the Roman community. Later, Pope Victor, (around the year 195) called for the convocation of synods— even in the Eastern territories—to try to bring some uniformity to this celebration of the resurrection. These synods were not successful, and the divergent practices still continued until the issue was settled at the Council of Nicaea with the agreement that Easter would always be celebrated on Sunday.[5] Important and illustrious synods were held in Africa in the third century. Of particular note are the great synods of Carthage in the time of St. Cyprian (258). It is quite clear, then, that the holding of synods did not begin with the Council of Nicaea or with the reign of Constantine. In fact, "By the third century…synods had become quite numerous in both East and West. Nor was the phenomenon of synodality restricted to the Empire, for there were also such synods held in the Church of the East, and also in the Armenian Church, both of these outside the Empire."[6] Thus, by the third century (well before Nicaea), synods had become universal and were being held even in times of persecution when imperial law forbade such gatherings.[7]

This clearly indicates that synods did not have their origin in Roman imperial polity. They arose out of a collegial instinct for apostolicity and communion. Synods "…were an expression of the fact that the Episcopal office itself must be assumed and exercised as something collegial in its very essence and in its origins, subject at least to some sort of review and confirmation by…authority transcending the local church."[8] The local church was integrated into the living communion of the neighboring and regional churches, and synods were events that expressed collegiality and communion. They were a witness of a deep and enduring conviction that the Church is one and that it is catholic and apostolic. In this pre-Nicene period, it was clear that whatever diversities existed had to be balanced by the claims of unity and communion.

How was the membership of pre-Nicene synods determined? The synods were not meetings of all the bishops of the Catholic Church. There was a regional quality to the membership. What determined the circumscription of the region? An important factor was that evangelization took place initially in metropolitan centers. These were centers of trade and travel. It was often in larger metropolitan centers, such as Antioch or Alexandria—and, of course, Rome—that Christian communities arose outside Jerusalem. It was from these centers that the faith spread into the outlying, rural areas and to smaller population centers. It was natural, then, that these outlying communities would look to the original community and to the bishop of that community for leadership and coordination among the derivative communities.

It is not surprising in light of this that, in addition to the synods as events, the metropolitan structure evolved in the Church very early, perhaps as early as the second century, before the organization of the empire into provinces by Diocletian (284–305).[9] The first stage, then, in developing structures of communion were the synods and the metropolitan structure.

An early documentary witness to the metropolitan structure is a collection called the Canons of the Holy Apostles.[10] Canon 34 states, "The bishops of each nation should recognize the one among them who is first and acknowledge him as head, and should do nothing extraordinary without his consent, each one doing only those things that pertain to his own community and the territories around it. Yet neither should the one who is first do anything without the consent of all; for thus there will be oneness of mind, and God will be glorified through Christ in the Holy Spirit."[11] It is significant here that the role of the head, *protos*,[12] is described not simply in terms of parliamentary order but that his role should lead the bishops to oneness of mind, reflecting the oneness of the Most Holy Trinity. This evocation of the Trinity also is the foundation for the reciprocity between the *protos* and the other bishops, neither of which is to act without the other. "The prerogatives of the *protos* somehow were regarded as necessary for the expression of the very nature and exigencies of episcopal collegiality" and were "rooted in the very nature of episcopacy, even though by definition they could be exercised only by certain members of the episcopate."[13]

Before the Council of Nicaea, then, synods were a normal way for bishops to deal with church issues. Also, before Nicaea — and even before Diocletian's reorganization of the Roman Empire into provinces and civil dioceses, there was a metropolitan structure functioning widely in the Church. This means that while all bishops were equal in holding the same episcopal orders (all were bishops), the *protos*, that is the metropolitan in this case, exercised a wider authority than the others. The first prerogative of the metropolitan bishop mentioned in the Council of Nicaea is that he is to confirm the election of bishops in his province.[14]

The Council of Nicaea also shows that at this very early period, individual bishops were accountable to other bishops. This is already implied by the fact that the election of a bishop was not merely a matter of the individual church community but involved the bishops of the province and was confirmed by the metropolitan bishop. But, also in disciplinary matters, the bishop was accountable. For instance, if an individual bishop enacted an excommunication, Nicaea required that it should be brought to the meeting of the bishops of the province. One reason for this requirement was to avoid a situation whereby "those expelled by some (be) admitted by others."[15] Another reason was to insure against such an act of a bishop being done out of "pettiness or quarrelsomeness or any such ill nature on the part of the bishop."[16] Clearly the bishops of Nicaea were marked by a consciousness of mutuality and communion in which there was a certain measure of accountability.[17] Nicaea decreed that provincial synods were to be held twice a year, which shows that these gatherings were not seen simply as responses to some unusual situation but as a normal structure of governance by bishops in a province.

CHAPTER 3

STRUCTURES OF COMMUNION: THE PATRIARCHATES

The fact that before the year AD 325, synods were held everywhere in the Church demonstrates that the bishops realized "no bishop was entitled to exercise his office in isolation from the common good of all the Churches, or from his brothers in the episcopacy."[1] Bishops understood that their judgments and acts were not the private acts of an autocrat. They were the judgments and acts of a bishop in communion. The monarchical episcopate—in the sense of a single bishop in each church—had become universal during the second century. And with this development, synods provided a counterweight to excesses in the exercise of episcopal authority by an individual bishop in his local church.[2]

The Council of Nicaea, however, shows that there was still a further development underway. A structure that would include more than one metropolitan province was taking shape. And so we read in canon 6 of Nicaea I, "The ancient customs of Egypt, Libya and Pentapolis shall be maintained, according to which the bishop of Alexandria has authority over all these places, since a similar custom exists with reference to the bishop of Rome. Similarly in Antioch and the other provinces the prerogatives of the churches are to be preserved."[3] Two things should be noted, however: The Council of Nicaea does not use the term *patriarch*, which was only to develop later. And the council did not create the patriarchal structure. Rather it refers to this arrangement of several provinces under the authority of a *protos* as already an "ancient" custom.[4]

The position of most scholars is that canon 6 is talking about what later was called a patriarchate and not just a large metropolitan province. The patriarchate consisted of several provinces with their metropolitan bishops. It was, therefore, the prerogative of the Bishop of Alexandria to ordain the metropolitans of Egypt, Libya, and Pentapolis. In this prerogative of ordaining the metropolitans lay the basis for the title patriarch: the Bishop of Alexandria was the father of the other fathers, the first father.

The Council of Nicaea mentions four sees as having a certain preeminence: Rome, Alexandria, Antioch, and Jerusalem, which in the canon is called Aelia.[5] Alexandria is the only one mentioned that has a specific territory identified. Canon 7 makes it clear that the bishop of Jerusalem did not have "the dignity proper to the metropolitan," but it is not clear that the authority of the bishops of Rome and Antioch extended at that time to a whole civil diocese. Nevertheless, the reality later known as the patriarchal office was making its appearance in the case of Alexandria.[6] In the case of Rome, the Bishop of Rome did exercise authority in central and southern Italy and the Italian islands. This was comparable to the authority exercised by the Bishops of Alexandria and Antioch.[7]

At this point (the early fourth century), what role did the *protos*, called the archbishop,[8] play in these groupings comprising several provinces? He presided at the regional synods and ordained all the metropolitans. But what principle lay behind this structural development?

It was not a drive toward conformity with civil territorial boundaries. We know this because Alexandria, which had authority over several metropolitan provinces, belonged to the civil jurisdiction of Antioch. What lay behind this whole development was a movement toward ever increasing unity, unifying the churches around a center. And the center was determined not so much by its civil prominence as by the fact that the center had been the origin of the other churches who shared its theology, spirituality, and liturgy.[9] Unity and communion lay behind the development of these larger groupings.

Canon 6 of the Council of Nicaea, then, is a recapitulation and a description of Church order. The council did not create or originate that order. It affirms that what would later be called the "patriarchal" ordering of the Church was an "ancient" tradition in regard to Alexandria. Magee maintains that it was the liturgical and spiritual traditions that gave rise to the patriarchates and that these, therefore, belong to the very definition of the patriarchate. However, other scholars see the origins of the patriarchates also in the recognition that, in larger territories, there had to be a *protos* (a head or first bishop) to serve the needs of order and communion among the churches. In fact, the first prerogative of the *protos* mentioned in the Council of Nicaea is the administrative act of confirming the election of bishops in the province.[10]

The patriarchal ordering of the Church has endured in the Eastern Orthodox Churches and in six of the Eastern Catholic Churches, namely the Coptic, Melkite, Syrian, Maronite, Armenian, and Chaldean Churches. In the Latin Catholic Church, the only patriarchate has been Rome. There were, in the first-millennium West, great metropolitan churches, such as Carthage in Africa or Arles in France. But the gathering of several metropolitan churches into a larger structure, a patriarchate, did not develop in the Western Church. The only see functioning as a patriarchate was Rome.[11] For many centuries, the pope had the title "Patriarch of the West." But Pope Benedict suppressed that title in 2006.[12] While it is not entirely clear why he did this, we do know that both Joseph Ratzinger and Yves Congar raised serious questions about whether the pope could function in any really effective way as Patriarch of the West in the modern world.[13]

As we have seen, the Council of Nicaea affirmed that the Bishop of Rome did have authority extending beyond the limits of his province and, over the course of the first millennium, this authority of the pope came to be recognized as extending over the whole Western half of the Roman Empire. But in the first millennium, there was a distinct difference between the way the popes exercised authority in the Western half of the Empire and the way they exercised authority in the Eastern half of the Empire. For instance, the popes appointed the bishops of Thessalonica as their vicars in the easternmost part of the Western Empire, but never attempted anything like that in the Eastern patriarchates. This fact is one of the reasons for describing the exercise of authority by the Bishop of Rome as patriarchal in the Western half of the Empire as distinguished from his exercise of truly papal authority in the matters concerning the whole Church, such as essential questions of doctrine.

But after the separation between the East and the West— usually placed around the year 1054, the popes exercised authority only in the West. Consequently, there was no longer any basis for a distinction between the patriarchal and papal exercise of authority. The result was that the exercise of papal authority in the whole Latin Catholic Church had the characteristics of patriarchal administration, and in the second millennium, this developed into a centralized papal monarchy.

With the discovery of the New World in the fifteenth century and the missionary expansion of the Latin Catholic Church in the sixteenth and following centuries, the patriarchal kind of papal government was gradually extended over the world-wide Catholic Church, bringing with it uniformity of liturgical language and practice, the choice and appointment of all bishops by the pope, and the appointment of papal delegates in all countries where the Catholic Church had been planted. And so, in practice, there was no longer any distinction between the patriarchal and the papal functions of the Bishops of Rome.

While the separation between the East and the West, and the missionary expansion beyond Europe, increasingly blurred the distinction between patriarchal and papal roles of the pope, another development was taking place that served to underline the difference between these roles of the Bishop of Rome. Since the twelfth century, when a group of Eastern Christians called Maronites formally reconfirmed their communion with Rome, there have been communities of Eastern Catholics who have continued to use their traditional liturgy and language and have continued to have a certain autonomy in the election of their patriarchs. The number and variety of such relatively autonomous churches in communion with the see of Peter increased as a result of the efforts of Latin Catholic missionaries to bring groups of Eastern Orthodox Christians into communion with Rome. Others, such as the Ukrainian Greek Catholic Church, on their own initiative, entered into visible communion with Rome. The presence of all these Eastern churches in the Catholic Church shows clearly that there is indeed a difference between the pope's exercise of *patriarchal* authority over the Latin Church where he appoints all the bishops and exercises other administrative authority, and his exercise of *papal* authority over the Eastern Catholic Churches in communion with Rome. This distinction has been made even more explicit by the promulgation of the *Code of Canons of the Eastern Catholic Churches* where the relative autonomy of these churches is upheld. It is not surprising, then, that Joseph Ratzinger would write, "Unity of faith is the pope's function; this does not prohibit independent administrative agencies like the ancient patriarchates." And he went on to say, "The extreme centralization of the Catholic Church is due not simply to the Petrine office but to its being confused with the patriarchal function which the bishop of Rome gradually assumed over the whole of Latin Christianity. Uniformity of church law and liturgy and the appointment of bishops by Rome arose from a close union of these two offices. In the future they should be more clearly distinguished."[14] It is evident, then, that both Congar and Ratzinger included the administrative dimension in their understanding of the patriarchal office. What is to be said, then, regarding the observations of Ratzinger and Congar about the need for new patriarchates on the basis of the fact that the present Latin Catholic Church, which comprises such a large portion of the globe, is increasingly unmanageable as a single patriarchal division? Both these theologians saw the weaknesses of what Ratzinger called "extreme centralization" when such a vast and diverse territory is involved.

It is an administrative problem because it is self-evident that a central authority cannot, in fact, adequately know and understand such vast and diverse cultures and territories. Cardinal Stephen Fumio Hamao of Japan, who had studied in Rome and later (after being Bishop of Yokohama) served for some years in the Roman Curia, pointed out in an interview that "Most people in the Roman Curia are European- and American-minded. They cannot understand the mentality of East Asia and the Far East."[15] Having had the experience of teaching Latin to the Crown Prince of Japan, the cardinal said, speaking of Rome's encouraging of the use of Latin, "It is impossible for Asians.... That is European-centered. It is too much!"[16]

There is no principle or doctrine of Catholic faith, nor any canonical provision that prevents the establishment of new patriarchal structures in the Latin Catholic Church along the lines of the Eastern Catholic Patriarchal Churches. Creation of such structures could be a way of solving what Joseph Ratzinger rightly called "extreme centralization." This would not only promote the inculturation of the Gospel but would, as well, open up a more effective way for evangelization. The Bishops of Japan, for instance, have said for many decades that their inability to attract many converts is due to the fact that they are made to present Christ with a Western face. Vatican Council II explicitly noted the link between the modern Episcopal conference and the ancient patriarchates.[17] How such structures might function in practice and what safeguards would be necessary to insure Catholic unity not only with Rome but among such different countries and cultures themselves could fruitfully be the subject of a carefully prepared deliberative papal synod. This might include not only an examination of the history of patriarchal structures in the Church, their strengths and weaknesses, but would necessarily envision how bishops would need to be prepared for such new structures in order to function effectively in them.

CHAPTER 4

STRUCTURES OF COMMUNION: MODERN CATHOLIC PATRIARCHATES

Patriarchal structures are and have been functioning in communion with Rome from ancient times to the present. They offer some indications of what could be possible in the Latin Church. The powers and functions of the actual modern patriarchates in communion with Rome are described in the *Code of Canon Law for the Eastern Catholic Churches*.[1] The Eastern Code describes the patriarch as "father and head" (55) of his patriarchal church. For this reason, he must always be mentioned in the liturgy after the pope (91). The patriarch must also show "hierarchical communion with the Roman Pontiff, successor of Saint Peter, through the loyalty, veneration and obedience which are due to the supreme pastor of the entire Church" (92). The patriarchal church comprises all metropolitans, all bishops, and all the faithful of that church (56). In the patriarchal church, there are four principal structures: the permanent synod (115), the patriarchal synod (102), the patriarchal curia (114), and the patriarchal assembly (140).

The permanent synod is made up of the patriarch and four other bishops who serve a five-year term. Three of these are elected by the bishops of the patriarchal synod and one is appointed by the patriarch (115:2). The permanent synod must be convoked at determined times but at least twice a year (120). An indication of the importance of the permanent synod is the stipulation that if, when the patriarchal synod is in session, a matter arises that belongs to the competence of the permanent synod, that matter will remain under the competence of the permanent synod (119).[2]

All bishops of the patriarchal church are members of the patriarchal synod. But with the agreement of the permanent synod, the patriarch can invite persons other than bishops, such as experts in certain fields, to give their opinion to the bishops gathered in the synod. The Eastern Code does not determine a fixed interval at which the patriarchal synod must meet, but it does say that it is to be convoked whenever the patriarch, with the agreement of the permanent synod, judges it necessary (106:2), or when at least one-third of the members request the convocation of the patriarchal synod (106:3). The patriarch prepares the agenda for the synod with the approval of the members, to which individual bishops can add other questions if they have the support of one-third of the membership. It is interesting that the patriarch convokes the patriarchal synod, but must have the agreement of the permanent synod. In addition, he must convoke the synod if at least one-third of the members request it. These are very wise provisions. The fact that he must have the agreement of the permanent synod is a brake on the arbitrary use of the power of convocation. It is also conceivable that the patriarch and the permanent synod together would oppose the convocation of the synod because they did not wish some issue discussed or did not wish a certain course of action to be approved. In such a case, at least one-third of the bishops have the authority to require the patriarch to convoke the synod and, thereby, to address issues of importance to the bishops.

The patriarchal synod makes laws for the entire patriarchal

church and carries out the election of the patriarch and of bishops. In other words, the appointment of bishops and of the patriarch is done in and by the patriarchal synod (110:3). The patriarch, following his election by the synod, is enthroned and assumes his office with the full effects of law (75, 77). It is after the patriarch has assumed his office that two other requirements must be fulfilled: the synod must dispatch a synodal letter to the pope, informing him of the election and enthronement; and the new patriarch must send a letter to the pope, asking for ecclesiastical communion. The election of bishops is also done in the patriarchal synod. But different from the election of the patriarch, the list of those elected must first be sent to Rome for approval. If a bishop is elected from that list, no further approval is needed. But approval of Rome is needed if the one elected is not on that list (180–89).[3]

The patriarch is bishop of a diocese, just as the pope is bishop of a diocese (Rome). As bishop of a diocese or eparchy, the patriarch will have a diocesan curia (administrative offices) to assist him in the government and pastoral care of his diocese. But the Eastern Code requires that, in addition to his diocesan curia, the patriarch have a patriarchal curia as well (114).[4] The patriarchal curia is comprised of the permanent synod, which is distinct from the patriarchal synod, and other officials who will be mentioned later. Members of the permanent synod are the patriarch and four bishops designated for a five-year term. Three of these bishops are elected by the patriarchal synod and one is appointed by the patriarch (115). The permanent synod must be convoked at determined times, at least twice a year (120).

In addition to the permanent synod, which is part of the patriarchal curia, the Eastern Code mentions three other members of this curia: the patriarchal finance officer, the patriarchal chancellor, and the patriarchal liturgical commission. The finance officer is required to have expertise in financial matters.

While named by the patriarch, the finance officer must also have the consent of the permanent synod and cannot be removed by the patriarch except with the consent of the patriarchal synod (122:1,2).[5] In other words, while the patriarch can appoint the finance officer only with the consent of the permanent synod, he cannot remove him without the consent of the larger body—the patriarchal synod. This provision, of course, gives a certain independence to the finance officer, enabling him or her to call policies or decisions to account without fear of reprisal. At the same time, the provision that the patriarch can remove the finance officer with the consent of the patriarchal synod means that the finance officer is also accountable and, if circumstances require it, can be removed (122).

The patriarchal chancellor is to be a priest or deacon and is appointed by the patriarch. He presides over the patriarchal curia and the archives of that curia. Nothing is said about involving the patriarchal or permanent synod in this appointment and nothing is said about any term limit on this appointment (123).

The Eastern Code attaches great importance to the liturgical commission. It says that every patriarchal church must have one and that its members are appointed by the patriarch (124).

In addition to the patriarchal synod, the permanent synod, and the patriarchal curia, there is the patriarchal assembly. This is of particular interest inasmuch as it includes participants who are not bishops or clerics. The Eastern Code states, "The patriarchal assembly is a consultative group of the entire Church over which the patriarch presides" (140). It then goes on to stipulate that this assembly assists the patriarch and the synod of bishops of the patriarchal church "in dealing with matters of major importance…"

Who are the participants in the assembly? There are two groups of participants: those who must be convoked and those who can be invited to participate (143). The Eastern Code mentions as mandatory invitees all the bishops of the patriarchal church, certain superiors of religious orders, rectors of Catholic universities and deans of theology and canon law, and rectors of major seminaries. In addition to these, from each eparchy (diocese) in the patriarchal church, at least one priest, one religious or member of a society of common life, and two lay persons must be invited. There can be a greater number of each category if the statutes provide for this. The assembly is required to have statutes and these must be approved by the synod of the patriarchal church (145).

Among the participants who can be invited are members of another Catholic Church who are permitted to take part in the proceedings in accord with the provisions of the statutes. Finally, observers may be invited from other churches or ecclesial communities. The patriarchal assembly, then, is really a gathering of the whole patriarchal church—bishops, priests, religious, and lay people. But can this assembly remain a dead letter? The Eastern Code states that the assembly must be convoked at least every five years and is, therefore, not left up to the arbitrary decision of the patriarch. It is mandated by the law itself. The assembly can be convoked more often than every five years, but in that case, the patriarch must act either with the consent of the permanent synod or of the patriarchal synod (141).

Canon 144 states that any of the Christian faithful "has the right to pose questions to his hierarch." The canon does not elaborate on this assertion but it certainly conveys the sense that, ideally at least, there should be great openness between the faithful and their bishops to the degree that the faithful may feel free—as a matter of right—to raise any issue with their bishops. Notwithstanding this declaration, the canon stipulates that only the patriarch or the patriarchal synod is to determine the matters to be discussed in the patriarchal assembly. In actual practice, some of the patriarchs or major archbishops send a letter to their clergy, religious, and faithful, inviting their suggestions concerning matters to be raised at the patriarchal assembly or synod of bishops.[6]

The patriarchates, as they have developed in history, are churches with a specific and distinctive identity formed and expressed by their liturgy, their spiritual heritage, and their customs. But this sketch of the modern patriarchate shows that there are also administrative dimensions to the patriarchates. Hence, the patriarchates cannot be said to consist exclusively of this spiritual and liturgical heritage. For example, the Maronite and the Syrian Catholic patriarchates both have similar liturgical traditions. The Ukrainian Greek Catholics and the Melkites also have similar liturgies. The question arises, then, whether new patriarchates could be created in the Latin Catholic Church, even if those patriarchates did not involve a specific spiritual and liturgical heritage proper to themselves. For example, Australia and New Zealand both share the Latin rite and a common spiritual heritage such as the monasticism of St. Benedict, the devotional life of saints such as St. Francis or St. Teresa of Avila, and devotional practices such as the Rosary and the Stations of the Cross. The Churches of Australia and New Zealand are not distinguished by a structure, liturgy, or spirituality different from the Catholic Churches of Japan, the United States, or France. The question is, then, whether these vast and manifold territories and churches could become autonomous churches in communion with Rome along the lines of the patriarchates of the Eastern churches.

Both Ratzinger and Congar maintain that, in modern times, it is the source of many problems for the pope to exercise a patriarchal role over a territory so vast and diverse as Japan, Australia, the United States, Latin America, Europe, and Africa. Both favor the creation of new patriarchal structures in the

Church. Ratzinger says, "And someday perhaps Asia and Africa should be made patriarchates distinct from the Latin church."[7] Congar takes an even broader view: "Is it possible…to imagine the structure of a reunited Church…in a collegiality of patriarchates: the five of the pentarchy, those of Moscow, Romania, Serbia and Bulgaria, and others yet to be created, for instance, Canterbury, Africa, Latin America, the Indies and others. Is this a utopia? Certainly not in view of the ecclesiology of the most ancient tradition."[8]

The Second Vatican Council, at which three popes had participated as bishops and one pope, Benedict XVI, was a theological consultant, envisioned the Episcopal conferences in some sense at least as a modern embodiment of the patriarchate.[9] The council did not go into the specifics about how this would be carried out in practice, and there are many things that would have to be determined, such as whether patriarchal powers would be confined within the Episcopal conference of a single nation or whether it would include large regions that have a single culture and are made up of multiple countries and Episcopal conferences. Whatever is to be said about the geographical configuration of new patriarchal structures, the linking of the ancient patriarchates with the modern Episcopal conferences certainly opens the way for Episcopal conferences to have a substantive role in three areas mentioned explicitly by Joseph Ratzinger: church law, liturgy, and the appointment of bishops.[10]

All things considered, then, it could be very beneficial for the whole Church and reinforce the unity and communion in the Church, if some of the aspects of the Eastern patriarchates were adopted in the Latin Catholic Church. It cannot be stated too often, of course, that such provisions cannot logically be rejected on the grounds that they are inimical to the primacy of the pope inasmuch as great and ancient Catholic Churches of the East have had all these prerogatives uninterruptedly from ancient times and faithfully embrace the primacy of the pope. Nor can such proposals be logically opposed on the grounds that they are an attempt to diminish the papal office, since they have been put forward in his published writings by one who is now, himself, holder of that office.

CHAPTER 5

STRUCTURES OF COMMUNION:
DELIBERATIVE SYNODS

At a press conference in October of 1965, a little less than six weeks before the end of Vatican Council II, Cardinal Paolo Marella, President of the Commission on Bishops and the Government of Dioceses at the Council, made the point that the recommendation for bishops to share with the pope in the government of the universal Church went back as far as the preparatory stages of the Council, as early as June of 1960.[1] It was not a matter of passing interest.[2] It will be instructive to see something of the development of this idea at Vatican II.

When the draft of the document on the Church (*Lumen Gentium*) came to the council floor for discussion and debate in the fall of 1963, a central issue was the doctrine of collegiality. Addressing this topic, several bishops raised the suggestion of creating a central representative body of bishops to assist the pope in the government of the universal Church.[3] In addition to this major document on the Church, there was another document also under consideration, which dealt specifically with bishops. But to the surprise of many, the conciliar commission assigned to draft the decree on bishops (*Christus Dominus*) never held a plenary meeting. Instead, Cardinal Marella appointed a small subcomission to prepare the draft for discussion and debate. This draft was not seen even by the official members of the commission itself until it was presented formally on the floor of the council.[4] Consequently, the draft was judged unsatisfactory and many bishops offered written observations and amendments prior to the actual debate on the floor. One amendment, submitted by an unidentified bishop, called for the establishment of what he called an "Apostolic Council" to be made up of bishops from all parts of the world. According to this bishop, such a council would be "a more perfect sign of the collegial rule of the whole Church," and would be a more effective means of promoting the common good.[5]

The draft, together with the amendments and observations of the bishops, was circulated and debate began on November 5, 1963. On the very first day of the debate, several bishops spoke supporting the idea of some kind of representative body to assist in the government of the universal Church.[6] This was a bit vague, of course, but it was quickly to become more specific. On the second day of the debate, Cardinal Bernard Alfrink of Holland, a Scripture scholar, offered the proposal for the creation of a central body, which would be a sign of the collegial rule of the whole Church. It would be more than a sign, however, because—as proposed by Alfrink—it would, in fact, exercise a collegial government of the whole Church together with the pope.

A still more specific proposal came from the distinguished Melkite patriarch, Maximos IV Saigh.[7] Like Cardinal Alfrink, he called for the creation of a body of bishops to assist the pope in the government of the universal Church. The draft document, prepared by Cardinal Marella, had proposed that some bishops might have a part in the work of the curia as consulters or members of some Roman congregations. But the patriarch scorned what he called this "timid little reform."[8] To restrict the participation of bishops to merely assisting in the work of the curia, said Maximos, did not respond to the needs of the times and could in no way be described as true collegiality.

Elaborating his ideas, Maximos then focused on the primatial role of the pope and enunciated this doctrinal principle: "If the Church has been entrusted in a special way to Peter and to his successors, it has also been entrusted to the Apostles and to their successors."[9] This doctrinal truth means that both the successor of Peter and the college of bishops have a universal role. Based on this truth, the patriarch then proposed that there should be created a synod that would meet at regular intervals, made up of bishops who were actually pastors of dioceses around the world, to take part with the pope in the universal government of the Church.[10] However, the patriarch pointed as well to another obvious and important reason for creating such a body. "The Holy Father," he said, "no more than any other person in the world whatever his talents, cannot govern an institution as large as the universal church just with the assistance of his own bureaucracy."[11] It is evident, then, that what Cardinal Alfrink and Patriarch Maximos were proposing was not the creation of an advisory body to the pope. They were proposing a body of bishops that would truly share in the general government of the Church.

The draft document on bishops moved forward containing a section that expressed the strong desire of the episcopate for such an international body. The draft explicitly stated that such a body would be a sign of the participation by all the bishops in the solicitude for the universal Church.[12] But two years were to elapse before the draft was presented to the council in the fall of 1965. This was the draft that, after all the discussion on the floor and the written amendments recommending a synod, caused some uneasiness because it made no explicit mention of a synod as such, although it did contain a paragraph expressing—in general terms—the desire that a group of bishops should assist the pope in the care of the universal Church. This surprise is understandable because there had been significant support in the council for a synod. For instance, the bishops of Germany and Scandinavia, more than a hundred bishops of Brazil, a number of bishops from the Philippines, several prominent French cardinals, and bishops from Indonesia and South Africa—to mention only some who spoke on this topic—favored the idea of a synod.[13] Among American bishops who spoke publicly on this topic was Archbishop Joseph T. McGucken of San Francisco. On September 19, 1964, the New York Times carried a lengthy report of a press conference held in Rome at the end of the first week of the third session of the council. According to this report, "The idea of a body to share the Pontiff's supreme authority over the church has long been discussed.…However, its imminence and its hierarchical superiority to the Roman Curia have never been stated more clearly and explicitly than by Archbishop McGucken."[14] The archbishop, referring to the decree on the Church then under discussion, stated, "If chapter 3 is passed, an imminent next step will be the establishment by the Holy See of some body (of bishops) working with him[15]—above the Curia."[16] This proposal and the widening support for it among bishops all over the world was greeted with growing alarm by prominent members of the Roman Curia, among them Cardinal Ottaviani, pro-prefect of the Holy Office,[17] and Cardinal Michael Browne, a member of the Holy Office. These redoubtable figures began by attacking the very foundations of collegiality. Cardinal Ottaviani stated that he had consulted an expert in Sacred Scripture who assured him that there was no scriptural proof that the apostles formed a college by divine institution. The *coup de grace*, tirelessly employed even today, was the grave accusation that those who advocate such collegial structures want to diminish—if not altogether abolish—papal primacy.[18] To reinforce this point of view, Cardinal Browne went on to say that the idea of a synod of bishops would be contrary to the dogmatic teaching of Vatican Council I.[19] Accordingly, he urged the bishops of the council to be on guard when such ideas arose.[20]

These, of course, are very serious objections. As for the collegiality of the apostles and of the bishops—their successors, this doctrinal truth is now established in the Church both in the teaching of the Second Vatican Council[21] and in the world of biblical and theological scholarship. It is also taught in the *Catechism of the Catholic Church*.[22]

The point had been made during Vatican II that such a council or synod would not be a novelty "since the Pope already had a council in the college of cardinals."[23] Before the sixteenth-century Council of Trent, the cardinals in Rome, in fact, did function as something of a permanent synod. They met three times a week to deliberate on important matters.[24] With the changes resulting from the Reformation, bishops were required to live in their dioceses and cardinals who were diocesan bishops had to observe this law of residence, making it impossible to continue the weekly meetings. A new arrangement came about, assigning the cardinals in groups called congregations to specific issues such as reform of the clergy or Catholic doctrine. When this arrangement began, the pope no longer met three times a week with the college of cardinals and similarities to a permanent synod disappeared. Since Vatican II, in addition to the members of the curia who live in Rome, there are other members who are bishops and archbishops of major sees, some of whom are cardinals, and who have the pastoral care of a diocese. These members do not reside in Rome, but they do take part in annual plenary sessions of the office or congregation[25] of which they are members, and they have a right to attend other sessions where business is to be done in which they have a special interest. These cardinals and bishops, by sharing in the work of the

Roman Curia, can be said (in some sense) to assist the pope in his day-to-day government of the universal Church.

But there is another kind of assistance bishops can and should be giving to the pope that would take the form of a deliberative synod. In this case, the bishops would not simply advise the pope about his primatial ministry. Rather, the bishops together with the pope would make decisions regarding matters of far-reaching importance for the universal Church. This kind of deliberative collaboration is not altogether novel. For many centuries in the first millennium, the popes convoked the Roman Synod whose members were the bishops of central and southern Italy. These were bishops who had the pastoral care of dioceses and could partake in the decision-making process of the synod in light of their actual and on-going experience as pastors.

In the Roman Synods of the first millennium, the synod (presided over by the pope) made important decisions concerning doctrine and such disciplinary matters as the deposition of bishops. This practice continued into the second millennium with the participation of bishops from the whole Western world. During the period of the Gregorian Reform,[26] momentous decisions were made in these synods, such as the enforcement of clerical celibacy, the prohibition of lay investiture, and the excommunication and deposition of Henry IV.[27] Gregory VII, among the very strong popes of history, held synods almost every Lent.[28] He attached great importance to these synods as instruments of reform.[29] "There is no suggestion in the sources that the bishops in the synod played a secondary role, merely ratifying decisions made by the pope. On the contrary, decisions seem to have been reached by means of debate in the synod."[30] The Roman synods were the forerunners of the medieval Western councils, which began with the four councils held at the Lateran between 1123 and 1215. The historical Roman Synod could, therefore, be a model for a modern deliberative synod. Such a structure stands in continuity with the long practice and history of the Church. And we should note that, far from diminishing the authority and role of the pope, the historic Roman Synods expressed the authority of the Petrine office, enhanced the unity of the Church, and promoted significant reform.[31]

Responding to the desires expressed by many bishops before and during the council, on September 15, 1965, Pope Paul VI established the synod of bishops by a formal decree. In doing so, he said, "…we should be profoundly convinced of the importance and the necessity of a broader use of the assistance of the bishops for the welfare of the universal Church."[32] In promulgating the norms for these synods, the pope said, "By its very nature it is the task of the Synod of Bishops to inform and to give advice. It may also have deliberative power when such power is given to it by the Sovereign Pontiff…"[33] In fact, no synod to date has been given deliberative power, and (as a consequence) the synods held since Vatican II have not been a sharing by bishops in the government of the universal Church but are rather a way for bishops to collaborate with the pope in his primatial function.[34]

What large numbers of the bishops at Vatican II desired was a means whereby they would share, as successors of the apostles, with the pope in the government of the universal Church. The law itself provides that a deliberative role may be given to synods by the pope. It would be most appropriate that a deliberative role be given to extraordinary synods, since they are made up of the presidents of Episcopal conferences in the Latin Church and the patriarchs and major archbishops of the Eastern Catholic Churches. Thus, they are bishops who not only have the care of a diocese, but have also been elected by their fellow bishops to positions of broader responsibility in their respective churches. For this reason, they would be well qualified to take part in deciding issues of greater importance affecting the life of the whole Church together with the pope. A deliberative synod finds its deepest roots in the teaching of Vatican Council II: "However, the order of bishops, which succeeds the college of apostles in teaching authority and pastoral government…is also the subject of supreme and full power over the universal church, provided it remains united with its head, the Roman Pontiff and never without its head…"[35] The bishops together with the pope have supreme and universal authority in the Church. A deliberative synod of bishops presided over by the pope would be a sign of the responsibility of the Episcopal college for the government of the whole Church. But a synod is not an ecumenical council and is not a subject of "supreme and full power over the universal church." What would be the grounds for this kind of synod having decision-making authority for the universal Church? The only way this would be possible would be for the pope to grant to the synod deliberative power so as to share with him the authority for making decisions binding on the whole Church, a possibility Paul VI mentioned when he created the synod of bishops. At the same time, it should be clear that a synod of bishops is the only group of persons qualified to receive such authority and exercise it with the pope, since only bishops "by divine institution have succeeded to the place of the apostles as shepherds of the church: and the one who hears them hears Christ."[36]

CHAPTER 6

PREEMINENT STRUCTURES OF COMMUNION: COUNCILS

None of the structures of communion mentioned so far in this book involve the whole college of bishops—synods, patriarchates, or even a deliberative papal synod. An ecumenical council, however, involves the whole Church. Based on the meaning of a Greek word *oikoumene*, which literally means "the whole inhabited world," *ecumenical* came to mean "universal." An ecumenical council, then, is a council that is universal—"binding upon of the whole Church, as distinct from diocesan or provincial or other councils of a more local authority."[1] It was not until over a hundred years after Nicaea I that this word *ecumenical* was used of councils. The Council of Chalcedon[2] in AD 451 was the first to describe itself as "the holy and great and ecumenical synod."[3] Chalcedon also determined the list of which previous councils were to be accepted as ecumenical: Nicaea I (325), Constantinople I (381), and Ephesus I (431).

The criterion for determining what makes a council ecumenical has undergone some changes over the centuries, and the criterion for ecumenicity in modern councils is not the same as for the councils of the first millennium.

For instance, the first seven councils, which took place

over a period of 462 years, beginning with the First Council of Nicaea in 325,[4] and ending with the Second Council of Nicaea in 787, are all accepted as ecumenical councils by the Eastern and the Western churches, both Catholic and Orthodox.[5] Yet all these councils were held in the east, in what is modern Turkey, and all of them were convoked by the Emperor and presided over by him or his representative.[6] Legates of the Bishop of Rome and a few bishops of the West were present at some but not all of these councils. How then could they be said to be ecumenical, involving the whole Church? The criterion cannot be who presided over them because the Emperor or his representative presided over them.[7] The criterion cannot be who participated in them because the participants were almost exclusively bishops of the Eastern half of the Roman Empire. And as far as the reception of these seven councils is concerned, Francis Sullivan notes, "In hardly any case can we speak of an absolutely universal reception."[8]

Many scholars think that since it was, in practice, impossible to have a strictly unanimous consensus of the episcopate, toward the end of the first millennium the consensus of the Pentarchy—the five great patriarchal sees of Rome, Constantinople, Antioch, Alexandria, and Jerusalem—came to be recognized as the criterion for ecumenicity. It was the bishops who belonged to the four Eastern patriarchates who actually took part in the councils, and so the consensus of their patriarchs was taken as a sign of the consensus of the bishops themselves. But it was only with the consensus of Rome that there was a consensus of the Pentarchy—five patriarchs. The pope usually called a Roman Synod of some Western bishops to deliberate with him on the basis of which he gave consensus to the decrees of a council held in the East. Thus when the Bishop of Rome received the decision of the councils together with the four patriarchs of the East, this consensus was understood to express the consensus not only of the individual patriarchs, but of the whole episcopate. The criterion of the consensus of the Pentarchy was certainly operative at the final council of the first millennium, the Second Council of Nicaea. [9] This amounts to saying that councils are ecumenical when they involve the participation or at least the reception by the churches of both East and West, and until the sixteenth century, the idea prevailed in the Western church that only those councils in which both East and West had taken part were ecumenical.[10]

The schism between the Eastern church and the Western church in the eleventh century made it impossible to use the long-standing criterion of the Pentarchy in the second millennium since the four patriarchs of the East were no longer in communion with the Bishop of Rome.

What, then, is to be said of those councils that did not involve the bishops of the Eastern church and occurred after the schism—such as, the medieval western councils? Bellarmine and Baronius were among the first to include these councils among the ecumenical councils[11]; yet, this position is not universally accepted. For instance, Pope Paul VI spoke of the Second Council of Lyons, held in 1274, as "the sixth of the general synods held in the west." He does not refer to it as an ecumenical council.[12] Francis Sullivan proposes an interesting approach to this question and says, "I see no reason for denying that a future council which would manifest restored communion between East and West, with the full participation of Orthodox bishops, would be a qualitatively more ecumenical council than any that has been held since the beginning of the Great Schism."[13] Nevertheless, he maintains that in light of the teaching of Vatican Council II, it would be necessary to hold that later councils—at least Trent, Vatican I, and Vatican II—are true ecumenical councils.

The reason for this position is that the Second Vatican

Council teaches that the Church of Christ subsists (continues fully to exist) in the Catholic Church in communion with the Bishop of Rome.[14] From this teaching, it follows that the college of bishops, which is the successor of the Apostolic College, continues fully to exist in the Catholic Church in communion with the successor of Peter. It is, further, the teaching of Vatican II that "the supreme power over the whole Church which this college enjoys is solemnly exercised in an ecumenical council."[15] It follows that, for Vatican II, an ecumenical council is one in which the college of bishops, together with the pope, solemnly exercises its supreme power over the whole Church.

The approval of the decrees of an ecumenical council by both the pope and the bishops, as well as their confirmation and promulgation by the pope, are prescribed by canon law as necessary for the decrees to have obligatory force: *The decrees of an ecumenical council do not have obligatory force unless they have been approved by the Roman Pontiff together with the council fathers, confirmed by him, and promulgated at his order.*[16] An ecumenical council, thus, becomes the preeminent structure of communion because it is only in such a council that the whole college of bishops exercises deliberative power with the pope in making legislative and doctrinal decisions binding on the whole Church.

Vatican Council II was a dramatic witness of a communion that was truly ecumenical—of the whole world. As we have seen at the great councils of the first millennium, there were almost no bishops from the Western part of the Roman Empire. At the Council of Trent there were only bishops of Europe.[17] In the early sessions, there were hardly two dozen bishops; at the later sessions, just a little over two hundred bishops were present.[18] At Vatican Council I, there were bishops from a wide variety of countries, and there were forty-six bishops of the Eastern Churches in communion with Rome. A little more than 6 percent of the bishops came from mission countries—such as, those in Africa or Asia, but all of them were Europeans (more than half of them French).[19] All in all, the total number of bishops at Vatican I came to between six hundred and seven hundred. This number varied from day to day because of sickness, death, or other reasons.[20]

Vatican Council II surpassed all other councils in the number of bishops and the universality of its makeup. There were more than two thousand bishops, the majority of whom were not European. They came from all continents and cultures, and there was a significant participation by bishops of the Eastern Catholic Churches. Of the bishops from dioceses in Asia and Africa, a considerable number were natives of those continents. Vatican II manifested the Church as a communion gathered together in one faith, around one Lord, and in the bond of unity and communion with the successor of Peter. Karl Rahner wrote, "…it seems appropriate and justified to regard Vatican II as the first great official event in which the Church came to be realized as a *world—Church*."[21]

On the opening day, October 11, 1962, something occurred that set a fundamental tone and direction for the whole rest of the Council. It was a moment when the bishops awakened to the truth that they had come to Rome as bishops—heirs of the Apostolic College—who, together with the pope, had a true authority and responsibility for the Church. After the opening ceremonies on October 11, several items were distributed to the bishops. First, a list of all those present at the council, more than two thousand names. Then, in addition to a copy of the regulations, there was a list of the members of the preparatory commissions[22] and ten cards on which each bishop was to vote for sixteen members of each of the ten commissions of the council. Of course, these bishops coming from all over the world did not really know one another, and, for many of them, the only practical course would be simply to vote for those who had already been on the preparatory commissions, which would be in effect to endorse the names desired by the Roman Curia.[23]

When they gathered two days later in plenary session on October 13, the bishops were instructed that they were to vote immediately by putting down the names of their choice. A senior French Cardinal, Lienart, who had been appointed by Pope Pius XI in 1930 and was greatly respected, took everyone by surprise by rising to propose that the vote be postponed so that the bishops could have time to consider the names and vote more responsibly. There was immediate and general applause, indicating that Lienart had grasped the thinking of the whole body. Given the wide backing for this, an adjournment was called, which led to another significant and far-reaching consequence: the bishops began by meeting in their various episcopal conferences to work on the names, and this led to a new sense of the place of the conferences. It was an early sign that the bishops were growing in the understanding that their role in a council is one of communion and participation, not simply of subordinate compliance. They were not simply advisors to the pope, but were sharers with him in apostolic responsibility for the whole Church. What might, otherwise, have seemed a secondary moment, was, in fact, a moment of great significance. It was a turning point, marking the world episcopate as conscious of its collegial role.

Vatican II is also a witness of the unique importance of the pope in maintaining and supporting the communion and collegiality of the episcopate.[24] This, too, was shown in the first month of the council when the topic of divine revelation was on the agenda. If the vote on members of the commissions showed a consciousness by the bishops of their role, the vote on the sources of revelation showed a consciousness on the part of the pope that he understood the primacy as including the role of cooperating with and supporting the bishops. The Doctrinal Commission under the presidency of Cardinal Ottaviani, pro-prefect of the Holy Office, had prepared a text entitled *The Sources of Revelation*.[25] A very large number of the bishops found fault with this document. After some discussion, there was a vote whether to end debate on this text. There were 2,209 votes cast, of which 1,368 were for ending discussion of the Ottaviani ver-sion. This was equivalent to rejecting that version altogether. But there was a technical problem. The vote to discontinue fell short by 105 votes of the two-thirds required by the rules of pro-cedure. In effect, this would mean that the wish of a sizeable majority of the council would be rejected. Pope John XXIII, recognizing the wishes of the vast majority, created a mixed commission made up of members of both the Doctrinal Commission, headed by Cardinal Ottaviani, and the Secretariat for Christian Unity, headed by Cardinal Bea, charging the com-mission to "emend the schema, shorten it, and make it more suitable…"[26] This was a striking instance of cooperation between the pope and the bishops, an instance where he worked in an authoritative but brotherly way with a sizeable majority of the bishops.[27] It was also "determining for the direction Vatican II would take from that moment forward. It was an intervention that ruled in favor of the prevailing sentiment in St. Peter's…it dealt a heavy blow to the control the Doctrinal Commission was trying to exert, and it was thus a major force in sending the coun-cil on a way of its own choosing.…The importance of the vote of November 20 and of the papal intervention on November 21 can hardly be exaggerated."[28]

The distinguished Oxford scholar and professor at Rome's Gregorian University, Norman Tanner, has this to say, "The councils restore faith in the capacity of human nature. The par-ticipants confronted great issues of their day and the supreme challenge—so much more difficult—of presenting the mystery of Christ to the people of their time. They faced them with courage and directness and generally produced remarkably well-thought-out statements in response…" He goes on to say that "the councils represent one of the great collective achievements of humankind."[29]

CHAPTER 7

CONCLUSION

This book began with a treatment of the Church as a communion from the beginning. History shows that there was a very early development of structures of communion before the fourth-century Council of Nicaea. I believe I have shown that such structures are not and have not been a repudiation of papal primacy, which itself has taken different forms over the centuries.

Those who see the need for such structures in the Latin Church are often impatient that they do not develop more rapidly. Sometimes, though, impatience springs from the failure to acknowledge that the earthly Church is not the heavenly Church. The earthly Church walks amid the changes and chances of this fleeting world, scarred, wounded, imperfect, a clay vessel carrying an immortal treasure. Gregory the Great, remarkable for publicly acknowledging his own personal failings, saw also that the Church itself bows under the weight of sin and weakness. The Church, he said, is called dawn. "Since dawn moves gradually from darkness into light, the Church…is fittingly called dawn….The dawn intimates that the night is over; it does not yet proclaim the full light of day. While it attenuates the darkness and welcomes the light, dawn holds both of them, light mixed with darkness."[1] The earthly Church is dawn.

No one member of the Church possesses the whole of the Gospel or all the virtues. Whatever our hopes and dreams, we must all wait and work—and be patient in the waiting, and preserve unity and charity as we walk the pilgrim path of faith in our little day of time. God works and can work as he wills even in circumstances that are not ideal. The resurrection accounts in John place great emphasis on the presence of Christ even in the tears and doubts and darkness of a troubled Church. Hence, the repeated question of the Risen Lord, "Why are you weeping?"

In one of the earliest documents of Christian history, *The Shepherd*,[2] there is a parable that describes the building of a tower, and we are told that the tower is the Church. At a certain point, the workers stop and the tower is left incomplete. The author of the work, Hermas, asks, "Why have the workmen left the tower incomplete?" The answer: "It cannot be brought to completion until the Lord comes…"[3] In a sense, then, there is no golden age of the Church. It is always being built and will not reach perfection "until the Lord comes."

The structures of communion dealt with in this book—traditional structures—show what is possible for the pilgrim Church as it waits "until the Lord comes."

NOTES

INTRODUCTION

1. Joseph Ratzinger, "Primacy and Episcopacy," *Theology Digest* 19, no. 3 (Autumn 1971): 206. This article is a translation of "Primat und Episkopat," a chapter in Joseph Ratzinger's work, *Das neue Volk Gottes* (Dusseldorf: Patmos Verlag, 1969), 121–46.

CHAPTER 1

1. Klaus Schatz, *Papal Primacy* (Collegeville, MN: The Liturgical Press, 1996), 17–18.

2. Francis A. Sullivan, SJ, *The Church We Believe In* (New York/Mahwah, NJ: Paulist Press, 1988), 34–65.

3. Joseph A. Fitzmyer, SJ, *The Acts of the Apostles*, The Anchor Yale Bible Commentaries (New York: Doubleday, 1998), 270.

4. Sullivan, *Church*, 38.

5. For example, Gal 2:15–21.

6. Raymond E. Brown, *Introduction to the New Testament* (New York: Doubleday, 1997), 307.

7. The element of revelation also enters here. God revealed to Peter that no human being could be considered unclean. But the revelation was brought to fulfillment in the actual pastoral experience of Peter's meeting with Cornelius and witnessing the outpouring of the Spirit on Cornelius even before he was baptized.

8. Fitzmyer, *Acts*, 555.

9. Brown, *Introduction to New Testament*, 306–7.

10. Fitzmyer, *Acts*, 543. He states, "It is, in effect, the episode in the early church that eventually leads to the convening of official councils of later date."

11. Norman P. Tanner, SJ, ed., "The Council of Nicaea," in *Decrees of the Ecumenical Councils*, vol. 1 (London/Washington, DC: Sheed & Ward/Georgetown University Press, 1990), canon 4:7.

12. Archbishop Peter L'Huillier, *The Church of the Ancient Councils* (Crestwood, NY: St. Vladimir's Seminary Press, 1996), 38–39.

13. Ludwig Hertling, SJ, *Communio: Church and Papacy in Early Christianity*, trans. Jared Wicks, SJ (Chicago: Loyola University Press, 1972), 28–36.

14. Tertullian died around the year AD 226.

15. In this book, I am dealing with structures of communion. But to do justice to communion in the Church, it would also be necessary to consider the foundation and source of all visible communion in the reality of the interior communion of the Church and the churches with the Father through the Son in the Holy Spirit.

16. This word *synod* derives from Greek and literally indicates a point at which multiple roads converge. Picking up on this meaning, synod has been used to designate a meeting of bishops who come together from various places.

17. Michael K. Magee, *The Patriarchal Institution in the Church* (Rome: Herder Editrice, 2006), 105.

CHAPTER 2

1. Magee, *Patriarchal Institution*, 108.

2. Ibid., 105.

3. Ibid.

4. R. A. Knox, *Enthusiasm* (New York: Oxford University Press, 1950), 33.

5. This is stated in the official letter addressed by the Council of Nicaea to the Egyptians. Tanner, *Decrees*, 19.

6. Magee, *Patriarchal Institution*, 105–6. The term "Church of the East" refers to ancient churches that were outside the territories of the Roman Empire, such as those that were located in what is now modern Iraq. Consequently, this terminology does not refer to the "Eastern Churches" as we commonly use that term today.

7. Magee, *Patriarchal Institution*, 106.

8. Ibid.

9. Ibid., 109–10. For the reorganization by Diocletian, see Peter Brown, *The Rise of Western Christendom*, 2nd ed. (Oxford: Blackwell Publishing, 2003), 54–58.

10. These canons are not from apostolic times. They are believed to date from the fourth century. *The Oxford Dictionary of the Christian Church*, 3rd ed., eds. F. L. Cross and E. A. Livingston (New York: Oxford University Press, 1997), s.v. "Apostolic Canons."

11. Magee, *Patriarchal Institution*, 120.

12. While this Greek word means *first*, the canon cited uses both words: *head* and *first*.

13. Magee, *Patriarchal Institution*, 113.

14. Tanner, *Decrees*, canon 4:7 (see chap. 1, n. 11).

15. Ibid., canon 5:8.

16. Ibid.

17. Today, there are relatively few explicit requirements for bishops of the Latin Church to participate in the provincial structure of their region. Yet prudence dictates a measure of interdependence and communication among bishops that does not support the idea of an individual bishop as a "lone ranger." The Second Vatican Council expressed an earnest desire that synods should "flourish with renewed strength" and added, "At the present time especially, bishops are often unable to discharge their office fittingly and fruitfully unless they do their work in

daily closer agreement and collaboration with other bishops." Tanner, "Decree on the Pastoral Office of Bishops," in *Decrees*, decrees 36–37:936.

CHAPTER 3

1. Magee, *Patriarchal Institution*, 121 (see chap. 1, n. 17).

2. Klaus Schatz, *Storia dei Concili* (Bologna: Edizioni Dehoniane, 1999), 19. Certainly, the question arises about how things might have been different in the development of the pedophilia issue in the United States if bishops had had a more defined sense of communion as shown in the ancient Church.

3. Tanner, *Decrees*, canon 6:8–9. Libya was separated from Alexandria by a vast expanse of desert. At the time of Diocletian, it was divided into "Upper Libya," which was called the Pentapolis, and "Lower Libya," simply called Libya.

4. Tanner, *Decrees*, canon 6:8–9. Magee, *Patriarchal Institution*, 122–23.

5. Tanner, *Decrees*, canons 6–7:8–9. The Emperor Hadrian decided to build a new Roman city on the site of the destroyed Jerusalem. It was called Colonia Aelia Capitolina, *Aelia* from the first name of the Emperor: *Aelius Hadrianus*.

6. Magee, *Patriarchal Institution*, 129.

7. Schatz, *Papal Primacy*, 32 (see chap. 1, n. 1).

8. The title "patriarch" had not yet appeared.

9. The very name *metropolis* means "mother city."

10. Tanner, *Decrees*, canon 4:7.

11. The title "patriarch" has been given to some bishops in the Latin Church such as Lisbon or Venice but it is purely honorary.

12. The title quietly disappeared from the 2006 edition of the *Annuario Pontificio*. When its absence was discovered, it caused considerable speculation. The Council for Promoting Christian Unity published a brief statement indicating that the title "Patriarch of the West" was vague from the beginning and had become obsolete and impractical. One reason lay in the mean-

ing of "West." In an earlier time, West meant the Western half of the Roman Empire, which included almost all of Europe. In the modern world, however, West would include Latin America, the United States, Canada, Australia, and a very large territory. The Council for Promoting Christian Unity made the point that rather than considering the West as a patriarchate, the Church now has a new ordering brought about through Vatican II in the episcopal conferences and multinational conferences, such as the European Conference of Bishops.

13. Yves Congar, *Église et Papauté* (Paris: Les Éditions du Cerf, 1994), 26. Also, while Cardinal Ratzinger was prefect of the Congregation for the Doctrine of the Faith, a member of his staff—the Franciscan Father Adriano Garuti—published a book in which he attacked the notion of the existence of a Western patriarchate: *Il Papa patriarca dell'occidente?* (Bologna: Edizioni Francescane, 1990).

14. Ratzinger, *Primacy and Episcopacy*, 206 (see intro., n. 1). This is an English translation of a portion of a chapter of the Ratzinger book, *Das Neue Volk Gottes*.

15. Gerard O'Connell (special correspondent in Rome, Union of Catholic Asian News), in discussion with the author, April 12, 2007.

16. O'Connell, discussion. The cardinal said that there might be some possibility of understanding a culture like India but that it was almost impossible for the American or European to really understand the mentality and culture of the far east, such as Japan.

17. Pope Paul VI, *Lumen Gentium: Dogmatic Constitution on the Church* (Second Vatican Council, 1964), 23. Tanner, *Decrees*, 868.

CHAPTER 4

1. *Code of Canons of the Eastern Churches* (Washington, DC: Canon Law Society of America, 1991). In this chapter, I

will cite the Eastern Code canons in parentheses in the body of the text. This Code of Canons of the Eastern Catholic Churches was drawn up by a commission appointed by the pope and was promulgated by the pope.

2. Nevertheless, according to canon 119, the patriarch and the members of the permanent synod can decide to remand the issue to the decision of the patriarchal synod.

3. There are tensions between Rome and the Eastern Catholic patriarchs because, in the case of bishops who are outside the patriarchal territory, the appointment comes from Rome. The patriarchs maintain that this is an inappropriate limitation on the role of the patriarchal synod and point to the fact that, in the case of Latin Western church bishops living in the patriarchal territories, they are not appointed by the synod but also by Rome, which seems to the patriarchs to be incongruous.

4. The pope also has two comparable structures: the Roman Curia, which deals with matters pertaining to the universal Church, and the Roman Vicariate, which deals with the Diocese of Rome.

5. The finance officer is described as "a member of the Christian faithful"; therefore, a lay man or woman.

6. The major archbishop does not have the title patriarch but, in most things, is the equivalent of a patriarch. See canons 151–52 of the *Code of Canons of the Eastern Churches*.

7. Ratzinger, *Primacy and Episcopacy*, 206 (see intro., n. 1).

8. Congar, *Église et Papauté*, 29–30 (see chap. 3, n. 13).

9. John R. Quinn, *The Reform of the Papacy* (Crossroad, New York 1999), 104.

10. Ratzinger, *Primacy and Episcopacy*, 206.

CHAPTER 5

1. Cardinal Marella mentioned this simply as a part of the history behind a section of the document on bishops that was on the agenda for the final session of the council.

2. Klaus Mörsdorf, *Excursus I, The Synod of Bishops*, vol. 2 of *Commentary on the Documents of Vatican II*, ed. Herbert Vorgrimler (New York: Herder and Herder, 1968), 214–15.

3. Robert Trisco, "The Synod of Bishops and the Second Vatican Council," *American Ecclesiastical Review* 157 (July–December 1967): 147.

4. Joseph Fameree, "Bishop and Dioceses and the Communications Media (November 5-25, 1963)," in vol. 3 of *History of Vatican II*, eds. Giuseppe Alberigo and Joseph Komonchak (Maryknoll, NY: Orbis Books, 2000), 117–18.

5. Trisco, "Synod of Bishops," 148.

6. That this topic came up at once when the debate began shows that it was prominent in the minds of the bishops.

7. Notable for its content, the speech of Patriarch Maximos was also notable for the fact that he did not follow the council rule requiring that speeches be given in Latin. Although he was accomplished in Latin, he spoke in French as a way of underlining that it was an Ecumenical Council, not simply a council of the Latin Church. The complete text of his speech is found in the Acts of the Second Vatican Council, *Acta Synodalia Sacrosancti Concilii Oecumenici Vaticani II, Pars IV* (Typis Polyglottis Vaticanis MCMLXXII), 516–19.

8. Section 5 of the draft had proposed that some bishops from different parts of the world should be added to the Roman Curia as consultants or even members of some curia congregations.

9. *Acta Synodalia*, 518.

10. Maximos also proposed a permanent synod of bishops always with the pope. This would have been a way of bringing more international participation into the government of the Church because, at the time of the council, the curia had not yet undergone the internationalization that later took place. Also, Maximos pointed out that the cardinals, heads of the curial departments, were historically members of the church at Rome —that is, they were pastors and deacons of the Roman churches.

He declared that the government of the universal Church should not be carried out just by the local church at Rome but should have a universal, international character that would be more evident in a synod of bishops from various parts of the world.

11. *Acta Synodalia*, 518.

12. Trisco, "Synod of Bishops," 150.

13. Morsdorf, *Excursus I*, 173.

14. Robert C. Doty, "Catholic Council Expected to Vote a Bishops' Senate…," *New York Times*, September 19, 1964.

15. I.e., the pope.

16. Doty, "Catholic Council," *Times*.

17. Here, I use the terminology of that time. The name of the congregation was later changed to the "Congregation for the Doctrine of the Faith" and its head is now called "prefect." At the time here described, the pope himself was the prefect of the congregation while its functional head, for this reason, was called "pro-prefect."

18. The full text of the Ottaviani speech is found in *Acta Synodalia Sacrosancti Concilii Oecumenici Vaticani II, Pars IV* (Typis Polyglottis Vaticanis, 1972), 625. Trisco, "Synods of Bishops," 154.

19. *Acta*, 626–27. The bishops of Vatican II clearly did not see collegiality as contrary to Vatican I since they taught collegiality and cited Vatican I in support of their teaching as in chapter 3 of *Lumen Gentium*, 22.

20. Trisco, "Synods of Bishops," 154. Trisco says that Browne "implicitly waved the flag of the danger of heresy."

21. *Lumen Gentium*, 22–23. Tanner, *Decrees*, 865–68 (see chap. 1, n. 11).

22. *Catechism of the Catholic Church*, 2nd ed. (United States Catholic Conference, 1997), 880.

23. Morsdorf, *Excursus I*, 173.

24. John R. Quinn, *Reform of the Papacy* (New York: Crossroad Publishing Company, 1999), 142.

25. In the terminology used in Rome, these offices and congregations are called *dicasteries* from a Greek word that means "bureau."

26. Usually dated from around the middle of the eleventh through the first decade or so of the twelfth century.

27. Schatz, *Papal Primacy*, 96 (see chap. 3, n. 2).

28. I. S. Robinson, *The Papacy 1073–1198: Continuity and Innovation* (Cambridge University Press, 1993), 123.

29. Ibid.

30. Ibid., 124. In the Lenten synod of 1074, Gregory VII did veto a decree concerning Henry IV, but there is little evidence, according to Robinson, that he habitually played this role.

31. See also Norman Tanner, SJ, *The Church in Council* (London, New York: I. B. Tauris, 2011), 60–100.

32. Walter M. Abbott, SJ, ed., Introduction to "Apostolica Sollicitudo," in *The Documents of Vatican II* (The America Press, 1966), 720.

33. Abbott, "Apostolica," 721. Also, canon 343 of the *Code of Canon Law* repeats this provision for a deliberative role by the bishops.

34. John P. Beal, James A. Coriden, and Thomas J. Green, eds. *New Commentary on the Code of Canon Law* (New York/Mahwah, NJ: Paulist Press, 2000), 454–55.

35. *Lumen Gentium*, 22. Tanner, *Decrees*, 866. This is repeated in the *Code of Canon Law*, canon 336.

36. *Lumen Gentium*, 20. Tanner, *Decrees*, 864.

CHAPTER 6

1. Tanner, *The Church in Council*, 180.

2. Chalcedon, a very ancient city founded around 680 BC, is now a district in the modern city of Istanbul.

3. Tanner, *The Church in Council*, 180.

4. Nicaea is now the modern city of Iznik in Turkey.

5. Tanner, *The Church in Council*, 177.

6. The emperor was the only one in the first millennium who could effectively convoke a council, and while he presided at them, he did not vote.

7. The Empress Irene presided at Nicaea II. Tanner, *The Church in Council*, 9.

8. Francis A. Sullivan, SJ, *Magisterium: Teaching Authority in the Catholic Church* (New York/Mahwah, NJ: Paulist Press, 1984), 59.

9. Ibid., 86.

10. Ibid., 59.

11. Ibid.

12. Ibid.

13. Ibid.

14. *Lumen Gentium*, 8. Tanner, *Decrees*, 854. See also Francis A. Sullivan, SJ, *The Church We Believe In* (New York/Mahwah, NJ: Paulist Press, 1988), 21–33.

15. *Lumen Gentium*, 22. Tanner, *Decrees*, 866.

16. *Code of Canon Law*, canon 341.

17. Schatz, *Storia dei Concili*, 223 (see chap. 3, n. 2).

18. Tanner, *The Church in Council*, 78.

19. Schatz, *Storia dei Concili*, 223.

20. Ibid.

21. Karl Rahner, *Concern for the Church*, vol. 20, *Theological Investigations* (New York: Crossroad, 1981), 78. In this essay, Rahner compares Vatican II with the profound change that occurred when the Church ceased to be a Jewish Church and moved into the Hellenist-Roman world. As then it moved from being only a Jewish Church to becoming a European Church, so at Vatican II it moved from being largely a European Church to being a world Church.

22. These were the commissions that had been at work during the period 1959–62 before the actual opening of the Council.

23. Giuseppe Alberigo and Joseph A. Komonchak, eds. *History of Vatican II* (Maryknoll, NY: Orbis Books, 1997), 2:26.

24. Vatican Council I had taught that one aspect of the primacy of the pope is to foster the unity of the bishops: Introduction to *Pastor Aeternus*. Tanner, *Decrees*, 811–12. See also Michael J. Buckley, SJ, *Papal Primacy and the Episcopate* (New York: Crossroad Publishing Company, 1998), 45–52.

25. The Latin title was *De fontibus revelationis*.

26. John W. O'Malley, *What Happened at Vatican II* (Cambridge, MA: Bellknap Press of Harvard University, 2008), 150–51.

27. Alberigo et al., *History of Vatican II*, 2:266.

28. O'Malley, *What Happened*, 151.

29. Tanner, *The Church in Council*, 115.

CHAPTER 7

1. Gregory the Great, *Moral Reflections on Job*, Bk 29:2–4.

2. The author of this second-century work is Hermas, about whom not much is known.

3. *SS. Patrum Apostolicorum Opera*, ed. Sixtus Colombo (Societá Editrice Internazionale, Torino 1954), *Similitudo IX*:V 681 (my translation). Also: *The Apostolic Fathers*, tr. Francis X. Grimm (New York: CIMA Publishing Co. Inc., 1947), Parable IX:5.